RUN THE River

Michael Burgess
Art by Guy Wolek

Literacy Consultants
David Booth • Kathleen Corrigan

Contents

Preface

During the 1600s and 1700s, a large number of people were forcibly brought from countries in Africa to the colonies and territories that would soon become the United States of America. These Africans were sold into slavery. They labored long hours for no pay and were treated as if they were property, not people. These Africans suffered horrendous treatment from their owners and from society at large.

This story is set in Virginia in 1851. It is a story about a family of enslaved people and the life-changing decision they made. It is also a small part of the story of the many enslaved Africans who helped shape the history of the United States.

Chapter 1

Run, Hany!

I kept moving my legs as fast as they would go, while I listened for Ma's voice again. In the dark of night, I could not see ten feet in front of me. All I knew was that we had to keep moving. We had no choice. So I kept listening for that whisper-shout Ma could do so well. It was loud enough for me to hear but soft enough so that no one else could — no one except Pa, who was running too, just a little behind me.

Before we left earlier that night, Ma and Pa had told me to remember three important things: first, keep quiet; second, keep running; third, keep listening for Ma's voice. I was only nine, but I knew I could remember those things. I also knew that if I didn't remember those things, something bad would happen — such as the bad things that had happened back on Master Wilson's farm.

"Just a little while longer, Hany!"

Ma and Pa had not told me where we were going. They had just said we would have to travel far away from the farm. We would have to travel far enough to be safe — maybe far enough to be free.

I didn't know much about the part of Virginia we were traveling across, but I knew that we were close to the river. When I wasn't hearing Ma's voice or my own heavy breathing, I could hear the roar of the water. It was a sound I loved.

Back on Master Wilson's farm, I had been one of the children ordered to help wash clothes in the nearby river. I used to like to watch the flowing river as I washed the clothes, wondering where the river was going in such a hurry and hoping and praying that I could go with it. When I told Ma what I had been thinking, she smiled sadly at me and then turned away. I knew she didn't want me to see her cry.

Just around sunset several days ago, while we were eating our stale cornbread after working long and hard all day, Ma said to me, "Hany, I know how tired you are, and your pappy and I are tired too. But I want you to be like that river you're always thinking about. I want you to be fast and strong."

I looked at her, scrunching up my forehead as I did when I was confused. She smiled at me, but this time she didn't turn away. She stared at me with her deep brown eyes and whispered, "Be ready to run like that river, Hany."

Chapter 2

"Stop there right now!"

I had fallen asleep thinking about Ma's words over and over. At the time, I didn't know what she meant about me running like the river. It wasn't until Ma and Pa woke me up and I saw their faces that I knew — we were running away.

They explained everything to me as quickly as they could. At first, I didn't want to go because I was so scared. I knew what had happened to the others who had tried to run away from the farm before. Ma and Pa never told me, but I had figured it out. But then I thought about the river and what Ma had said about it earlier, and I put that fear all the way down in my feet, as Pa had taught me to do whenever Master yelled at me.

And I ran.

But now my legs were hurting and my chest was burning, and my mouth was so dry I wanted to jump right into the river and swallow it up. I did not think that I could keep running. I turned around to look for Pa. He had told me to run between him and Ma so that I would be safe. I guess he thought that Master might come after us too. Pa was there behind me, of course, and close enough for me to see him.

He must have seen the fear in my face because he ran a little faster, scooped me up, and slung me over his shoulder.

We caught up to Ma, and between breaths, Pa gasped, "Ruth, we can't run all night. We have to stop."

Ma shook her head and replied heatedly, "No, Isaac! We have to get as far away as we can while it's still dark."

I felt Pa get tense, as if he were about to bark right back.

Then I heard a powerful voice bellow, "Stop there right now!"

Only it wasn't Pa's voice.

Chapter 3

Uncle Henry

First Ma and then Pa, still holding me, stopped dead in their tracks. Along the river that we had been following were some small trees and bushes. The voice we heard was coming from behind a thicket not far away from where we stood holding one another and trying to catch our breaths. The moon seemed to be glowing brighter than before, so we were able to see a shape crouching behind one of the bushes.

Pa growled, "Who's there?"

Ma gently grabbed his arm to calm him because she knew that Pa would do anything to protect us. "Henry," she asked, "is that you?"

"Yes," the voice answered. "Is it really you, Ruth?"

The shape approached from behind the bush and ran to hug Ma. Ma opened her arms and hugged him right back. I looked up at Pa and saw he was smiling, so I knew it was going to be all right.

"Henry, you gave us a scare," Pa said and then gave this man named Henry, who I didn't know, a great big hug himself.

Henry looked down at me and put his hand on my head, saying, "Well, who is this pretty young lady? This couldn't be Hany, could it? 'Cause the Hany I last saw was a tiny little thing!"

"I *am* Hany," I replied. "Now, who are you?" I was trying to sound like a grown-up, but really I was still scared and confused.

"Hany!" Ma scolded.

"That's all right, Ruth. I can tell she's strong — just like her parents. Like me too! I guess we got that from our mammy and pappy, didn't we, Ruth?"

I didn't know how to read or write, since Master Wilson wouldn't let me do any learning, but I was still smart. Smart enough to deduce that Henry was kin.

"Hany, I'm your Uncle Henry — your mammy's brother — and I'm here to help you all."

"I figured that out all by myself," I said. "So where are we going now? I don't like it out here in the dark."

Pa nodded and said, "I agree."

Henry — Uncle Henry now — stretched out his long arm and pointed, replying, "Norfolk." He added, "And you know once Master finds out you all are missing — if he hasn't already — he's going to come looking. So let's go!"

Chapter 4

Norfolk

We made it to Norfolk by daybreak. Uncle Henry and some of his friends shared a home there. It was small and didn't have much furniture, but I felt safe just being there. Uncle Henry took us to the part of the house where everyone slept and told me to put my head down in his bed. He told Ma and Pa to get some sleep as well, and though they argued that they had too much to talk about with him, they must have been as exhausted as I was because their argument didn't last long.

When we woke up, Uncle Henry was sitting in a chair with his head in his hands. He looked exhausted, but more than that, he looked as if something was troubling him. I stayed in my bed and kept my eyes closed about halfway. When I heard Ma get up, I turned the other way so that she couldn't see my face. She could always tell when I was pretending to sleep. I knew she would ask me to leave the room so that she and Uncle Henry could talk.

Ma asked, "Henry, what's wrong?"

Henry took a deep breath and said, "Ruthie, it's still hard. We started off with something, but now I feel as if we have nothing. They don't let up."

"The whites?"

Uncle Henry nodded and continued, "When I first got this house after buying my freedom, I figured I could start a real life, and at first, I could. We had a real strong community of free black folks here. Now, they keep changing the laws to make it harder for us to make a living."

"At least you're free, Henry. Remember, we are still enslaved. They call us runaway slaves. And you know if Master Wilson ever finds us … Well, I don't even want to think about it."

That safe feeling I had disappeared quickly.

On the way up to Norfolk, Uncle Henry, Ma, and Pa had talked and talked. They talked about how Uncle Henry had been sold to another master because Master Wilson didn't trust him and how he had somehow saved enough money to buy his freedom from his new master.

They talked about something called the Underground Railroad and how Ma was able to find out that Uncle Henry would meet us somewhere along the river. They talked about this new law they called the Fugitive Slave Act, which made it illegal for free people to help enslaved people who'd run away, and how this law was dangerous, especially since we were considered fugitive slaves.

And now they were talking about how being a free black and being an enslaved person were just about the same thing. It didn't make a whole lot of sense to me, but it did bring back that feeling of terror I had tried to suppress.

Pa woke up, and overhearing Ma's conversation with Uncle Henry, he reprimanded us, saying, "Hush, you two! We don't want Hany to hear any of this."

Ma said, "She's still sleeping, Isaac. But you're right, and we should consider what to do next."

With quiet confidence, Uncle Henry responded, "I've got that covered, Ruthie."

Chapter 5

The Boat

Norfolk was a bigger city than I had ever been in. Walking around in the middle of the day with everyone looking at me — at least I thought they were — made me nervous. I had never been in a place with so many white folks. There were black folks as well, but I could tell pretty quickly who was in charge of the city. White folks could walk around minding their own business, with nobody bothering them or watching them, but it was different with black folks. People might not have been watching me, but they sure were watching Ma, Pa, and Uncle Henry. And a lot of those folks watching my family didn't look too happy to see us.

Uncle Henry said, "Now you can see that we aren't really free. I have my papers to show that I bought my freedom. I paid a good sum for those, but they don't do me much good when most of the people around here don't care about those papers."

Pa looked around for a moment before saying in a hushed voice, "Then why not come with us, Henry? Why not find a better life up north? That's what we're hoping for."

"Because I need to stay here and do what I can to help others. I figure, even if I am not truly free, I can help others try to be."

Ma put her hand in Uncle Henry's and said, "You always took care of me, Henry. You're a good man."

"Well, Ruthie, you were always worth it." Uncle Henry put his other hand in my hand and looked at me. "And you're worth it now more than ever."

After walking for a good bit, Uncle Henry stopped and said, "There she is."

We all looked out toward the Atlantic Ocean, following Uncle Henry's gaze. I realized that he was talking about the gigantic boat docked just a short distance away. Earlier, he had explained that we

would be getting on board a large boat — this boat, I now figured — so that we could sail north to a place called New York City.

New York was a free state, so we had a better chance of making a life there, Pa had said. That had brightened my day for a while.

But now that we were standing just a short way away from that huge boat, I felt that nervous feeling again — until I took a look around. Most of the people walking around this part of Norfolk looked like me. There were not a lot of people staring in our direction.

"Uncle Henry, what happened to all the white folks? Where did they go?"

Uncle Henry laughed, "Well, young lady, most of the crews on these ships are made up of blacks. Most of the free black neighborhoods are nearby as well. That's going to be a big help to us when we get you on that ship. It's due to leave tomorrow morning. All we have to do is make sure you are here on time."

Ma said, "We will do whatever we need to. We owe you so much, Henry."

"You don't owe me a thing. You're kin, and that's enough. Besides, I'm not the only one helping you. The captain of that ship, Captain Fountain, has been helping enslaved people get north for a while now."

I gasped and said, "That ship has a black captain?"

Uncle Henry laughed again. "No, he's a white man. But Hany, not all white people like the idea of slavery. That's one big reason you are heading north. Folks up there seem to be more opposed to the idea of slavery. It's getting a little harder now that the Fugitive Slave Act has more people on the lookout trying to capture escapees, but there are others who want nothing more than to help enslaved folks. In fact, word is that people up north want to put an end to slavery altogether."

"I like how that sounds."

All at the same time, Ma, Pa, and Uncle Henry said, "Me too!"

Chapter 6

A Chance

"H_{any!}"

I was dreaming about being on a boat on a river with Ma, Pa, and Uncle Henry. We were drifting slowly, just looking around at all of the beautiful trees and animals along the riverbank.

"Hany!"

I guess I'd have to dream another night. Pa was shaking me, so I knew I must have been in a deep sleep. I lifted my head, rubbed my eyes, and looked at Pa. His eyes were like two full moons.

"We've got to go right now!"

I knew something was wrong when I noticed that it was still nighttime. We were supposed to get on the boat in the morning.

"What's wrong, Pa?"

"No time to explain, honey. Your Ma and Uncle Henry are already out the door. You and I have some catching up to do."

Pa took me by the hand and lifted me up in a way that let me know he was serious. We left Uncle Henry's house carrying only our few supplies.

I could see Ma and Uncle Henry just up ahead. We ran to them.

"We need to find you a safe place to stay for the next couple of hours," Uncle Henry said. "The ship leaves just after sunrise, and you will not miss it if I have anything to do with it."

Uncle Henry led the way, sneaking behind the other houses in the neighborhood, staying off the main path. The houses didn't give much shelter. The four of us had to stay squeezed together to keep hidden. Uncle Henry was just about to move out from behind one house when he quickly ducked back out of the moonlight and into the dark again.

He put one finger to his lips. I closed my mouth as tight as I could. I was so scared I thought my fear might jump right out of my mouth as a scream. Pa wrapped his arms around me, trying to keep me calm and warm in the cool night. Uncle Henry peeked back out and then waved us on, and we all moved to the next house. It was there that he finally spoke.

"Hany, there are some people here who are looking for you and your mammy and pappy. These people are not nice people. They want you to go back to Master Wilson's farm."

"I don't want that!"

"I know, and that's why it's real important that you listen well. I know you're scared, but you need to be — "

"Fast and strong?"

"Exactly! Like an ocean wave."

"Or a river," Ma added. She gave me a smile that warmed me right up.

I looked at Ma and Pa and Uncle Henry, and I knew I would be all right.

Uncle Henry led us to a small building with lots of pieces of wood and different tools in it. He said it belonged to a carpenter, who was a friend of his. That let me know that he was one of the people who liked to help enslaved folks like us. We crouched down on the floor, out of sight of the door and windows.

"You should be safe here. When the sun rises, you go right out that door and walk straight to the ship," he told us.

"You have to go now, I suppose?" Ma asked, though I knew she already knew the answer.

"I do, Ruthie. I have to go make sure that the men who are looking for those three fugitive slaves find them."

My mouth dropped open.

He continued, "Yes, I believe I saw them traveling west toward the Appalachians. They were heading to Ohio, last I heard." Then he looked at me and winked, and I let out a little giggle.

Uncle Henry hugged Pa and Ma good-bye. Then he looked at me for a long time and said, "Hany, I hope I get to see you again someday. I know that you are going to grow into a very special person." Then he added, "Matter of fact, you already have."

I squeezed Uncle Henry so tight I thought I wouldn't be able to let go. When I finally did, I watched him slowly stand up and peek out a window to make sure it was safe. Then I watched him open the door and leave.

Ma, Pa, and I sat there together for what seemed like forever, waiting for the sun.

When the light started streaming through the windows, my heart lifted, but just a little. First Ma stood up, then Pa joined her once we heard the bustle of people getting to work and heading to the ship. We took one another's hands and walked out the door.

I had to ask, "Are we really going to be all right?"

Ma answered, "Hany, I won't make promises to you that I can't keep for sure, but we will do everything we can to try."

Pa said, "And no matter what, we will have each other."

"And a chance for something better, Hany," Ma added.

The sun shone down on us as we walked toward the ship and toward the hope of a better life — not just for us but for everyone who wanted nothing more than to be free.